$10.95

J
599.74   Ahlstrom, Mark E
AHL   The Black bear

THE BLACK BEAR

BY
MARK E. AHLSTROM

EDITED BY
DR. HOWARD SCHROEDER
**Professor in Reading and Language Arts
Dept. of Elementary Education
Mankato State University**

PRODUCED AND DESIGNED BY
BAKER STREET PRODUCTIONS
Mankato, MN

CRESTWOOD HOUSE
Mankato, Minnesota

CIP

LIBRARY OF CONGRESS CATALOGING IN PUBLICATION DATA

Ahlstrom, Mark E.
  The black bear.

  (Wildlife, habits & habitats)
  SUMMARY: Describes the physical characteristics, habits, and natural environment of the black bear, the most common bear in North America.
  1. Black bear--Juvenile literature. (1. Black bear. 2. Bears) I. Title. II. Series.
QL737.C27A48   1985   599.74'446   85-22872
ISBN 0-89686-276-3 (lib. bdg.)

International Standard Book Number:	Library of Congress Catalog Card Number:
Library Binding 0-89686-276-3	85-22872

ILLUSTRATION CREDITS:

Charles Palek/Tom Stack & Assoc.: Cover
Lynn Rogers: 5, 11, 12, 17, 18, 19, 21, 25, 27, 28, 31, 32, 35, 37, 38, 42, 44
Lynn Stone: 6
Warren Garst/Tom Stack & Assoc.: 9
Phil & Loretta Hermann: 14
Jim Brandenburg/DRK Photo: 41

CRESTWOOD HOUSE

Hwy. 66 South, Box 3427
Mankato, MN 56002-3427

TABLE OF CONTENTS

Introduction 4
The importance of teeth

Chapter I: A general look at the black bear 7
The black bear came from Asia
A wide range
The smallest North American bear
Black bears come in many colors
Normally timid animals
A smart animal

Chapter II: A closer look at the black bear 19
Looks different than a grizzly
The amazing eating machine
A special fall feast
Foods for all seasons
Bears cover a lot of ground
The senses
Small talk
Black bears have few enemies
A long winter's nap
Cubs are born during the winter
The cubs grow up
The future looks good

Map: 45
Index/Glossary: 46-47

INTRODUCTION:

The importance of teeth

Biologists believe that long ago the black bear ate only meat. The experts believe that these bears originally had cutting teeth like a wolf has. As the black bears' supply of prey animals got smaller and smaller over thousands of years, their diet changed. And so did their teeth. The bears' teeth slowly became flat on top. This made it possible for them to eat things other than meat.

While the black bear is still classified as a carnivore, or meat-eating animal, this does not give a true picture of its eating habits. Only about one-fourth of its diet is meat. Most of the time it eats plants and other vegetable matter. In reality, the black bear behaves like an omnivore, or animal that eats both meat and plants.

It's interesting to note what a little thing like teeth can mean to a wild animal. The wolf eats almost nothing but meat, and it has large sharp teeth to kill its prey. There is also no question that the wolf is much smarter than any bear. And yet, the wolf is in danger of becoming extinct, while bears are increasing in number. How is this possible?

American black bears have adapted very well to changes in their habitat.

Black bears eat many kinds of plants. This bear is eating "rose hips" — the fruit on wild roses.

Since the wolf's teeth force it to hunt and eat prey animals, it is often in conflict with farmers. As wilderness areas disappeared, wolves started to eat domestic livestock. The wolves had no other choice. Their natural prey had disappeared with the wilderness. People fought back by killing the wolves in great numbers. The wolf's teeth have caused the wolf nothing but trouble. Because bears have teeth that allow it to eat plants, it doesn't have to eat livestock. The black bear's teeth have allowed it to survive.

Let's now take a look at how the black bear has been able to live quite well in our civilized world.

CHAPTER ONE:

The black bear came from Asia

Very few wild animals have as wide a range as members of the bear family (called the family *Ursidae* by biologists). Some type of bear lives in almost every area of the Temperate Zones of the earth.

Biologists have divided the bear family into seven different types. They are the spectacled bear, the only bear in South America; the sloth bear, found only in India and Ceylon; the sun bear of southeast Asia, the smallest bear; the Asiatic black bear, found in the Himalaya Mountains between India and Tibet; the polar bear, which lives all around the North Pole; the brown bears (grizzly bears are a kind of brown bear), the largest members of the bear family; and the American black bear.

North America has polar bears, brown bears, and American black bears (from now on in this book we'll call this last type, "black bears"). Black bears are, by far, the most common of all North American bears. While no one has figured out a foolproof way to count bears, biologists can make some good guesses. They think that there are less than twenty thousand polar bears left in the world. Only part of these are in North

America. Between the grizzly and the Alaskan brown bear, there are maybe twenty-five thousand brown bears in North America. Biologists think that there may be as many as a half million black bears! It's no wonder then, that when most people think of bears, what they have in mind is the black bear.

Called *Ursus americanus* by biologists, the black bear is the smallest in size of all North American bears. It is also the only North American bear found only in North America. Brown bears and polar bears are found in Europe and Asia, too. What is interesting is that the black bear came from Asia. Thousands of years ago, in fact, black bears were found only in Asia. Like many other wild animals, they slowly migrated to North America. Biologists believe that they moved across a strip of land that once connected Asia to North America. Called the Bering Land Bridge, this strip of land is believed to have connected Russia with the state of Alaska.

Before we move on, it might be interesting to note one other fact. It is a surprise to most people to learn that bears are the dog family's closest relatives. (The dog family includes pet dogs, wolves, coyotes, and foxes.) Experts have discovered a link between dogs and bears. They found a fossil of an animal that lived a very long time ago. Called a "half-dog," the animal had features of both a bear and a dog. The experts believe that some of these animals slowly changed into members of the dog family, while others changed into members of the bear family. If you stop to think about it, even some pet dogs do look a lot like bears. Especially, if you took away their tails and added a couple hundred pounds!

A wide range

While the black bear slowly died out in Asia thousands of years ago, it did very well in its new North American home. Starting in what is now Alaska, it moved into almost all areas of North America. In fact, its original range was probably the largest of any big animal in the world. Its territory included (and still does) all but the most northern areas of Alaska and Canada. There were once at least a few black bears in every state

The black bear once had the largest range of any big animal.

of the lower forty-eight states of the U.S. And their range extended well into Mexico.

For hundreds of years the Native American Indians had hunted the black bear for its hide and meat. A large black bear has a great amount of fat, which the Indians mainly used to make lamp oil and cosmetics. The hides were made into bearskin "rugs," which were used for bedding and sometimes clothing. Even the claws and teeth of the black bear were used to make jewelry.

When the white settlers came to North America, they also hunted the black bear for many of the same reasons. As more and more settlers came, black bears started to disappear. Hunting did not cause this to happen, however. Instead, it was the cutting down of the forests and clearing the land that was the problem. Black bears need forests in order to survive. Before long, there were very few black bears in the eastern half of the United States. The same thing happened in the southern parts of Canada when forests were cut down for lumber or to grow crops.

The black bear continued to do well in all parts of North America that were hard for settlers to reach. This included the mountain regions of the eastern United States and all of western North America. It also included swampy areas that no one wanted to farm.

Today, most black bears are found in Alaska and in the states and provinces of western North America. There are also a large number of these bears all across southern Canada, in the states around the Great Lakes,

Black bears need forests to survive.

in the Appalachian Mountains of eastern North America, and along the Gulf Coast from Texas to Florida. In addition, the Ozark Mountains of Arkansas are home to many black bears.

To the surprise of many people, black bears are making a comeback in many areas that are being replanted with trees. For example, there is a reforested area in the state of New Jersey that once again has a good population of black bears. These bears live just across the Hudson River from New York City!

The smallest North American bear

Even though the black bear is the smallest type of bear found in North America, it is certainly big enough to be dangerous. The average adult black bear weighs three hundred to four hundred pounds (136 - 181 kg). Most adults are between twenty-seven and thirty-six inches (69 - 91 cm) tall at the shoulder, and between fifty-five and sixty-five inches (1.5 - 1.8 m) long from nose to rump. The males, called boars, are usually quite a bit larger than females, which are called sows.

Adult black bears usually weigh three to four hundred pounds.

Some very large black bears have been killed through the years. Sam Ball of Batavia, New York, shot a black bear in 1975, that weighed just over 750 pounds (340 kg). The largest-known black bear was shot near Stevens Point, Wisconsin, in 1885. This bear weighed 802½ pounds (364 kg). The longest black bear on record was killed near Milford, Pennsylvania, by Herman Crokyndall. This bear, which was shot in 1923, weighed only 633 pounds (285 kg), but it was nine feet (2.7 m) long. That's a lot of black bear!

Black bears come in many colors

Black bears were given their name because the first ones seen by biologists were black in color. These bears lived in eastern North America. Today, most of the black bears living in the East are still black, or at least very dark in color. Many of them have a patch of white fur on their chests.

In other areas of North America, however, black bears are almost any color except black. Experts now know that these other black bears developed different colors of fur to help them blend in with their habitat.

The black bears of the East are black because they live in heavy, dark forests. Black bears in the West live in more open areas, so their fur is lighter in color. The bears that live in the semi-open forests of the western mountains of North America are mostly brown or reddish-brown in color.

Two special types of black bears live along the Pacific Coast of southern Alaska or northern British Columbia. These bears often find themselves living the year around near the snow and ice of glaciers. One type, called a glacier bear, is often a bluish-gray color. The other type, called the Kermode bear, is white or cream colored.

Cinnamon-colored black bears are sometimes found in western North America.

Because these two types of black bear are very rare, they are prized trophies to hunters. Game managers, however, limit the number of these bears that may be shot. They don't want these special black bears to become extinct.

Normally timid animals

Black bears are normally very shy. Whenever they meet people in the wild, they will usually turn and run away. Contrary to myth, even a female bear with cubs will run away if she is given a chance. However, if the female is surprised, or if people get between her and her cubs, she will put on quite a show. The female may growl and snap her teeth together. This action is a warning for the people to leave! More often than not, the female will attack to protect her cubs.

Black bears have also been known to attack people in the wild for no apparent reason. The best guess that the experts can make is that the bears mistake people for other bears moving into a bear's territory. This is especially true during the summer mating season, when people are most likely to be in the woods. The experts also think that the bears are more likely to attack when there is a shortage of the bear's natural food supply. It's just a matter of competition—the bears don't want other bears or people to get "their" food.

Two things make the problem worse than it has to be. People think of black bears as friendly cowards, and people have gotten into the bad habit of feeding the bears. These two problems are common in national parks. Despite warning signs that tell people not to feed the bears, it seems that very few people can resist. The bears, of course, like the idea. For them, it's a free lunch. The bears get in the habit of coming for the handouts. People often think the black bear is cute and cuddly. They forget how close they are to danger. People think that grizzly bears and polar bears are dangerous, so they keep their distance from these bears. The result is that black bears have attacked and killed more people than any other North American bear.

A smart animal

Black bears are among the smartest of all wild animals. This ability has made it possible for the black bear to survive very well living near civilization. Unlike most other large wild animals that need large wilderness areas, bears are not bothered by being near people. In this respect, the black bear is like the whitetail deer, which has also thrived while living near people. The opposite is true of grizzly bears and mule deer—for a number of reasons, these animals don't do well when people move into their territory.

As whitetails have learned that it is easier to walk into a farmer's cornfield than it is to forage for acorns, black bears have learned that garbage dumps provide an easier meal than looking for berries. Like the white-tail deer, black bears have also learned to hide from man. Both of these animals are able to hide themselves so well, that people are often not aware of their presence. When living in the wild near people, black bears and whitetails have learned to do their feeding at night. It is only in wilderness areas and national parks that the black bear feeds during the day. In the parks, the bears feed during the day because they have learned that they are in no danger from people. They feed during

People have gotten into the bad habit of feeding black bears in parks.

Black bears have learned to find food in rural dumps.

the daytime in wilderness areas, because that is what they naturally prefer to do. In short, these clever animals have the ability to pick the safest, easiest route to survival.

Now that you know some general things about the black bear, it's time to look at some of the details of their day-to-day living habits.

CHAPTER TWO:

Looks different than a grizzly

How can you tell if the brown-colored bear you're looking at is a grizzly or a black bear that happens to be brown? Sometimes it's not easy, but there are a couple of clues that can help.

The first thing to check is the shape of the bear's face. To do this, you have to wait until the bear turns its face sideways. After the bear turns so you can see the profile of its face, look at its nose. Black bears have a "Roman nose." Their noses run in a straight line from their foreheads. If you laid a ruler from the tip of their noses to the top of their foreheads, everything in between would be in a straight line. (Note: this is just an

Black bears have a "Roman nose."

example—don't even **think** about doing it on a bear that is alive!) Grizzly bears, on the other hand, have a bit of a "ski-jump" nose. Their noses turn up, and come away from their foreheads at an angle.

A second thing to check is the area above their shoulders. The grizzly has a very definite hump that rises above its shoulders. This hump is sort of like the hump that a bison, or buffalo, has between its shoulders. The black bear does not have a hump.

A third thing to check is the paw print that the animals make. If you can find a paw print in soft dirt, you might be able to figure out some more things. If the track is close to twelve inches (30 cm) long, it was made by a grizzly. No black bear has a paw that large! If there are no claw marks showing in the paw print, it was probably left by a black bear. While the claws of a large black bear will sometimes show in soft dirt, the claws of a grizzly almost always will. This happens because the grizzly's claws are quite a bit longer than the claws of a black bear. With both types of bears, the smaller prints in a track are made by the front paws of the animal. The larger prints are made by the back paws.

If the bear you are watching is in a tree, there are some more things to know. If the bear is very large, it is probably a black bear. Adult grizzly bears are too big to climb into trees. Their claws are not strong enough to support their great weight. Adult black bears, however, have no trouble climbing trees. The black bear is the only North American bear that climbs trees as

Even large black bears have no trouble climbing trees.

an adult. If the bear is small, it could be either a grizzly or a black bear. The young of both types climb trees with ease.

The amazing eating machine

The black bear has forty-two teeth. Its front teeth are sharp enough to tear meat. The molars are flat on top, like a cow's teeth. This makes it possible for the bear to also grind-up and eat grasses and other plant materials.

The black bear has often been called a four-footed garbage disposal. The reason is obvious. These bears are able to eat just about anything that crosses their path.

Black bears have been known to eat some strange things. They've been seen eating briars, clam shells, ants, bark, roots, and mice. When tearing apart a beehive to get at the honey, the bears will often eat the whole hive!

In the spring, black bears eat grasses, many kinds of buds, and the soft, inner bark of evergreen trees. Later, they will dig up the bulbs of plants that form under the ground.

When berries start to ripen in the summer, the black bears eagerly search for them. In their haste to eat, they pull entire bushes into their mouths with their large paws. They eat not only the berries, but also the leaves of the plant.

People should be careful whenever they are in a blueberry patch. There is a very good chance that they could come face-to-face with a black bear! Blueberries are one of the black bear's favorite foods.

In the fall, black bears eat any ripe fruit that they can find. Apples are another of their favorites. The bears have no trouble finding wild apple trees or abandoned apple orchards. If there is a shortage of food in the wild, black bears will even come into small towns or the edges of big cities to get apples out of backyards and orchards.

As you can imagine, a large black bear can make quite a mess of an apple tree. The bears are not happy to eat just the apples that they can reach from the ground. Using their paws, the bears pull on any large branches that they can reach. This often breaks the branches. If the bears are really hungry, they'll also climb up into the trees. Just the weight of the bears breaks more branches. And when they get up into the tree, the bears will again pull branches towards themselves, breaking even more. Even a small group of bears can ruin a large number of apple trees in a hurry.

Another favorite fall fruit is acorns from oak trees. Black bears will eat acorns from all types of oak trees. Given a choice, the bears seem to prefer the acorns from white oak trees. Even to a human, these are the sweetest acorns. Experts believe that acorns provide most of the black bear's winter fat supply. Years ago, chestnuts provided the winter fat supply in the eastern United States. But a disease killed almost all of the chestnut trees in the early 1900's. In states east of the Mississippi, the black bears had to switch to acorns and beechnuts to fatten up for the winter.

A special fall feast

There is a special fall food for which black bears on the west coast of North America search. From Oregon, all the way to Alaska, many kinds of salmon make spawning runs. The fish move into rivers from the Pacific Ocean to spawn each fall. (Note: in the most northern areas, the spawning run starts in the late summer.) In these coastal areas, both grizzly bears and black bears are waiting for the fish. The bears "show up like clockwork" to enjoy the feast!

On the large rivers, there will sometimes be hundreds of bears. The bears wade in, almost forming a net across the shallow areas of a river. Some of the bears dive under the water, catching the salmon with their mouths. Others swipe at the fish with their paws, hooking the fish with their sharp claws. Still others use both their paws and their mouths to catch the salmon. Whatever their method, the bears are very good at catching the fish. They really stuff themselves with the rich meat! In these parts of North America, it is the salmon that give the bears a good layer of winter fat.

Foods for all seasons

As black bears walk through their forest habitat, they are always on the lookout for a quick snack. They will turn over rocks and logs looking for ants and other bugs. They will dig into the ground with their large paws if they locate mice, ground squirrels or chipmunks. And they will eat eggs and the young of birds that nest on the ground.

A black bear rolls a log, looking for bugs to eat.

If a black bear can get past the mother animal (which often is not easy), it may kill and eat the young of big-game animals. Black bears have been known to eat young moose, elk, caribou, mountain sheep, and deer. These bears are also able to kill adult big-game animals that are weak from old age or disease. A black bear will eat any dead animals that it finds, too.

It certainly is no myth that black bears love honey. Any honeybee hive that the bears walk by is in big trouble! In the wild, honey bees usually make their hives in hollow trees. Black bears are able to rip the trees apart to get at the sweet honey. Once the hive is exposed, the bears will eat the whole thing, wax and all. Any bees caught in the hive will also be eaten. The bees, of course, will try to sting the bear. Except for its nose, and small areas around its eyes, the bear is protected by its thick fur. Experts think that stings inside their mouths don't affect black bears. Which is a good thing, because there is a report of one black bear that had two quarts (almost two liters) of bees in its stomach!

If there is a shortage of wild honey, black bears will go after a beekeeper's hives. A single black bear can put a beekeeper out of business in a hurry. If ripping apart a tree is a little work, taking apart the wood boxes that beekeepers use is almost play to a bear.

If there is a shortage of natural food, black bears will sometimes get in the habit of killing pigs and sheep. Once the bears learn how easy it is to kill these animals, it's a hard habit to break. This is specially true of pigs, since pork is very tasty to a black bear. Once a bear begins to kill domestic livestock it might continue, even when it has plenty of natural foods. Game departments will try to trap these bears and move them to a new area. If the bear can't be trapped, or if it comes back, the farmer is often given permission to shoot the bear.

A final source of all-season food is the rural dump. Black bears have learned that rural dumps are an easy place to get food of all kinds. If there are any black bears living around a dump, they will show up almost

Rural dumps furnish an all-season supply of food.

every day at sunset. The bears paw through the garbage, eating almost anything.

The garbage doesn't seem to do the bears any harm. In fact, the bears seem to thrive on it. But the situation is not a good one. These ''dump bears'' have become a tourist attraction in many rural areas. All too often, people get careless. These bears have learned not to fear people. They don't run away when people drive their cars into the dumps. The bears will often let people walk up to them. Foolish parents sometimes take

"Dump bears" have lost their fear of people, and can be dangerous.

pictures of their children standing only a few feet from the bears. It's the same thing that happens in national parks where bears have become "tame." People must remember that no wild animal is ever completely tame. At any moment, a black bear could lunge and take a swipe with its paw. Disaster could strike at any time!

Bears cover a lot of ground

Black bears usually walk very slowly on all four feet as they search for food. If they have to, they can run very fast. They have been clocked at speeds up to thirty miles (50 k) per hour. Sometimes they will stand up on their hind legs to reach for food. They will also stand up to get a better view of what is ahead. Black bears can easily swim across lakes and rivers.

If a black bear decides to go up a tree to get food or to escape from a pack of wolves, it can climb very quickly. The bear digs in its claws and goes up the tree in a series of bounds. It's almost a running action! When the bear comes down, it comes down rump first.

Except for the few bears that have dumps to supply them with food, black bears have to wander over a large area to find their food. Many of the adult males wander over an area of fifteen square miles (38 sq. k). The males, or boars, are almost always alone. The females, or sows, cover less area if they have cubs to watch over. The cubs aren't strong enough to cover so much ground. The sows are also usually alone, or with their cubs.

Once a black bear gets used to its home range, it doesn't want to leave. Bears that are trapped and moved, because they caused trouble, will often return to their home range. It's common for black bears to find their way home after being moved thirty miles (48 k) away. The state of Michigan trapped several bears in an attempt to transplant them into new areas. Two of the bears didn't like being moved. One bear traveled almost one hundred miles (161 k) to get back to its home range. The other returned from about sixty miles (97 k) away.

The senses

In order of importance for survival, the black bear's sense of smell is most important. Its sense of hearing is second in importance, and its sense of sight is third.

The black bear uses its nose to find almost all of its food. Whether plants or small animals, the bear uses its nose to find its favorites. The black bear can smell and find dead meat or a dump that is several miles away. Their noses also warn them of danger from their enemies, which are mostly people.

Black bears use their sense of hearing to warn of danger from a distance. Their ears are the largest of all North American bears. The bears' ability to hear well usually allows them to either hide or leave, long before danger comes near. Many a bear hunter has learned this the hard way. A hunter can spend days in the woods trying to sneak up on a bear. The hunter might even know that there are several bears in the area, because they are in the local garbage dump every night. Only rarely will a hunter be able to sneak up on a bear and shoot it. This is why some hunters use dogs to track black bears. Other hunters put out a "bait" of the bears' favorite foods. These hunters wait nearby, hoping the black bears will come to the bait.

There is some question about how good the black bear's eyesight is. Even the experts can't agree. Some say that the bear's eyesight is not very good, and they

Mainly, black bears use their senses of smell and hearing to detect danger.

have stories to prove their point of view. Other experts say just the opposite. They think that at least some black bears have very good eyesight. And they, too, can tell of things that seem to prove it. It's probably safe to say that black bears have average eyesight.

The experts do agree on one thing—black bears don't need good eyesight to survive. Their senses of smell and hearing are enough. Some people even joke that a black bear could be blind, and still live for many years! It just might be true.

Even without good eyesight, a bear could probably live a long time.

Small talk

Not many people have heard the sounds that black bears make. That's because they only make sounds when they are around other bears, or threatened by danger. And when they do "talk" to each other, it's not with loud sounds. They don't howl like a wolf, or bugle like a bull elk. Elk live in herds, and wolves live in packs. These animals need to stay in touch. Black bears, on the other hand, prefer to live by themselves. They have no need to make loud sounds.

When adult bears are together during the mating period, they may growl, snarl, snort, grunt, or roar. The bears will make similar sounds to warn other bears away from their territory. If threatened, black bears will strike their teeth together, making a popping sound. Cubs whimper and whine much like human babies. The cubs will even cry when they are scared. Sows talk to their cubs with quiet coughs and grunts. They warn the cubs of danger with a loud grunt. If a boar should wander too near the cubs, the sow might pop her teeth at him. The sow knows that a boar might kill the cubs, if she doesn't warn him to stay away.

A black bear that is hurt or wounded will sometimes groan and moan. These sounds are very much like the sounds that a person in pain would make.

Black bears have few enemies

Except for man, black bears have few, if any, enemies. They are generally too big and strong to be bothered by other animals. About the only time they get in trouble is when they are weak from sickness or old age. A pack of wild dogs or wolves could corner a bear that is weak. By attacking and biting the bear's legs and stomach they can slowly kill the bear. Even so, the bear would probably get in a few swipes with its paws, wounding its attackers. Because dogs and wolves know how dangerous even a sick bear is, they will usually wait for the bear to die on its own.

Most of the time, all a black bear has to do to avoid being attacked is to climb a tree. Usually the dogs or wolves get bored after awhile and leave. Then the bear comes down from the tree and goes on its way.

If black bears go after the young of big-game animals they can be badly injured by the mothers of the young animals. Big-game animals, such as elk and caribou, can use the hooves on their front legs with surprising speed and power. Many a bear has learned this the hard way. While the hooves will seldom kill black bears, they will certainly leave a painful reminder. Unless the bear is starving, one blow from a hoof will usually cause it to run away.

Black bears are bothered by a large number of very

tiny enemies. Biologists know that there are at least twenty-five parasites, like ticks, lice, tapeworms, and lungworms, that make life miserable for bears. Like pigs, they can be infested with trichinae—the tiny worm that can cause trichinosis in humans. (This is why pork and bear meat has to be well cooked to be safe for people to eat.)

Parasites are seldom fatal to black bears, but some diseases are. The bears can be infected with rabies, tuberculosis, and some forms of pneumonia. These diseases will usually cause the bears to die.

The black bear's worst natural enemies are probably other black bears. There are often terrible fights during

This sow and her cub have climbed a tree to get away from danger.

the mating season. These fights can lead to injuries that later cause death. If there is a food shortage, boars will sometimes kill cubs. Grizzly bears have also killed adult black bears when their ranges overlap. Because adult grizzly bears are so much larger, black bears are no match for them.

Man can be an enemy for two reasons. When forests are cut down, black bears can no longer survive. The bears need forest habitat to get their food. The bears cannot keep moving to new forest areas. An area can only support so many bears with food. The result is fewer bears. The second reason is when people's activities cause the black bears to lose their fear of man. Many bears have had to be killed because we have made them tourist attractions in dumps and national parks. Black bears and people just don't mix. Sooner or later a bear will do something we think is wrong or dangerous, and the bear will have to be killed.

Bear hunting today is usually used only as a way to control the number of bears in an area. The hunting is very carefully controlled by game departments throughout North America. Hunting is allowed only when there are too many bears. If the hunters didn't kill the bears, the bears would start doing things that people don't like. They would start coming into small towns looking for food, or killing farmer's livestock. The bears have to do this in order to survive. Bear hunters enjoy their sport, and killing some of the bears serves a useful purpose.

A long winter's nap

The average black bear lives about fifteen years in the wild. A few bears are known to have lived for twenty-five years. The oldest bear on record was thirty years old. For wild animals, even fifteen years is an old age.

Perhaps the black bear's secret to living so long is the long nap that it takes every winter. It may come as a surprise to learn that bears don't really hibernate. Black bears do not fall into a deep sleep like woodchucks and some other animals that truly hibernate. Instead, they are "dormant" during the winter. They do spend

Black bears spend most of the winter in dens. This bear woke up when the photographer got too close.

This photo shows a black bears den at the bottom of two large rocks.

38

a lot of time dozing or sleeping, but they can become active in an instant when bothered. In areas of southern North America that don't get very cold, the bears don't hibernate at all.

Having fattened up during the summer and fall, the black bears start to get drowsy when the weather turns cold. They begin to look for a winter den. The den can be in any place that is sheltered from the weather. The bear might find a spot under a pile of rocks, or under the roots of a large tree that has been blown over. If the bear is lucky, it might find a small cave or abandoned mineshaft. Most dens will be on the north side of a hill or mountain. If it's not too cold, some bears might just decide to curl up in a dense thicket of small trees.

Most bears will carry a large amount of leaves and grasses into their dens to make a soft bed. Pregnant females will usually take special care to see that their dens are large and comfortable. The females will give birth during this winter period.

Before going into their dens for the winter, most black bears will quit eating. They will get rid of all materials in their digestive tract. The bears than eat leaves, pine needles, and sometimes, a bit of their own hair. These materials form what biologists call an "anal plug." The plug usually stays in place all winter, helping the bear to keep its den clean. Black bears get rid of the plug when they come out of their dens in the spring.

A sleeping bear's temperature stays close to normal during the winter. The bear "feeds" itself by consuming the layer of fat that it built up. Many black bears start the winter with a layer of fat that is five inches (12.8 cm) thick. The layer of fat on a large boar could weigh as much as two hundred pounds (91 kg)! The bears often wake up to change positions.

Most black bears will come out of their dens sometime in March. The first thing a bear does when it comes out of its den is to drink a lot of water. Experts believe that this is to soften their digestive system. Before long, they are eating the first grasses and buds that sprout in the spring.

Cubs are born during the winter

Black bears mate during June and July. The mating season is the only time that the adult males and females are together. The older boars do most of the breeding, and they may mate with more than one sow. Sows have to be in their fourth year before they are ready to mate for the first time. The mating is brief, but almost tender. The black bears may "kiss" each other with their tongues. They rub against each other, and often stroke each other with their paws. Once mating takes place, the boar leaves.

Sows carry their young for about seven months. The cubs are born in the female's den in late January or early

Dr. Lynn Rogers, an expert on black bears, drugged this sow so he could safely study her three-week-old cubs.

February. Sows that are pregnant for the first time will usually have one cub. In later years, they will usually have two cubs. It's not unusual for older sows to have three or, even, four cubs. As many as six cubs have been reported.

Most cubs weigh about one-half pound (.2 kg) when they are born. The bodies of the cubs are covered with very fine hair. Their eyes are closed, and their tiny ears lie flat against their heads. Very small claws show on the tips of their toes. The cubs are too helpless to do anything except nurse and sleep.

The cubs open their eyes for the first time when they are about forty days old. Thick fur begins to cover their bodies, which now weigh about four pounds (1.8 kg). Two months after the cubs are born, the sow takes them out of the den for the first time.

The cubs are ready to come out of the den when they are two months old.

The cubs follow their mother as she hunts for food, night and day. They stop often to rest. The cubs nurse many times each day, and sleep after each feeding. Before long, the cubs start to sample some of the same foods that their mother eats. The cubs spend most of their time wrestling and playing. If they get out of line, the sow swats them with a paw. If danger threatens the cubs, their mother sends them up into the nearest tree. The greatest danger is from a large boar. The sow will fight the boar if she has to, but usually she can frighten the boar away by growling and popping her teeth.

The cubs grow up

By October, the cubs will weigh nearly fifty pounds (23 kg). They will have a big layer of fat, just like their mother. In December the sow and her cubs will go into the same den together. When the group of bears come out of their den in the spring, the cubs are very hungry. They are no longer nursing, and eat any food they can find. By their second June, the cubs will weigh about eighty pounds (36 kg).

If the group meets a boar, the sow will not chase him away this time. Instead, she will leave with the boar to mate. The cubs are now on their own.

The cubs will usually stay together into the fall. They

will often spend the winter together in the same den. But when spring comes for the third time, they will go their separate ways. In a couple years, the female cubs will be having cubs of their own.

The future looks good

Because the black bear has been able to survive while living near people, it will probably continue to do very well in the future. As long as people provide forest areas, there will be plenty of black bears for everyone to enjoy.

The future looks good for the American black bear.

MAP:

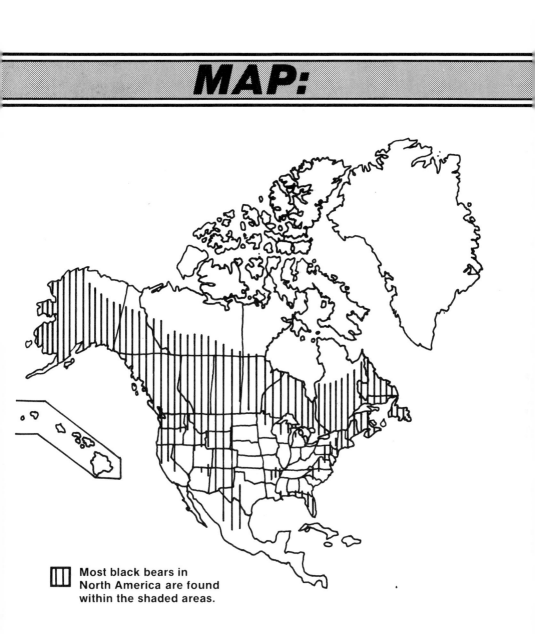

Most black bears in
North America are found
within the shaded areas.

45

INDEX/GLOSSARY:

BEEKEEPER — *26 A person who raises bees to make honey.*

BERING LAND BRIDGE — *8 A strip of land that once connected Russia with Alaska.*

BIOLOGIST — *4, 7, 8, 13, 35, 39 An expert on plants and animals.*

BOAR — *12, 29, 33, 36, 40, 43 An adult male bear.*

CARNIVORE — *4 A meat-eating animal.*

COLORING — *13, 14*

CUB — *15, 29, 33, 36, 40, 41, 42, 43, 44 A young bear.*

DEN — *37, 38, 39, 40, 42, 43, 44 The home of a wild animal, usually dug into the ground or side of a hill.*

DIET DISEASES — *00, 00, 000*

DOMESTIC LIVESTOCK — *6, 26 Tame animals that are raised by farmers.*

DORMANT — *37 To be mostly inactive.*

ENEMIES — *30, 34, 35, 36*

EXTINCT — *4, 15 No longer living anywhere.*

FORAGE — *17 To look for, and eat, natural foods.*

FOSSIL — *8 The remains of plants or animals from an earlier age.*

HABITAT — *5, 13, 24, 36 All of the things that make up the area where an animal lives.*

HIBERNATE — *37, 39 To sleep through the winter.*

HOME RANGE — *29 The area in which an animal lives.*

MATING — *33, 36, 40, 43, 46*

MIGRATE — *8 To leave one place or region and live in another.*

MYTH — *15, 25 An old story or legend that is not true.*

OMNIVORE — *4 An animal that eats both plants and animals.*

PARASITE — *35 An animal that lives in or on another animal, getting food from it.*

PREY — *4, 6 An animal that is eaten by other animals for food.*

RANGE — *7, 9, 10, 36 The area in which a wild animal can naturally survive.*

SENSES — *30, 31*

SIZE — *8, 12, 13*

SOUNDS — *33*

INDEX/GLOSSARY:

SOW — *12, 29, 33, 40, 41, 42, 43 An adult female bear.*

SPAWN — *24 The method by which fish reproduce—males fertilize eggs deposited by females.*

TEMPERATE ZONES — *7 The areas of land between the tropical and polar regions.*

TRANSPLANT — *29 To move something from one area to another.*

TRICHINOSIS — *35 A disease caused by a parasite that lives in pigs and bears.*

WILDLIFE
HABITS & HABITAT

READ AND ENJOY THE SERIES:

If you would like to know more about all kinds of wildlife, you should take a look at the other books in this series.

You'll find books on bald eagles and other birds. Books on alligators and other reptiles. There are books about deer and other big-game animals. And there are books about sharks and other creatures that live in the ocean.

In all of the books you will learn that life in the wild is not easy. But you will also learn what people can do to help wildlife survive. So read on!